Praise for
Wrenwyck Williams

"*Baby Food*" *is an easily digestible and nourishing book for your soul. When you feast your consciousness on the principles offered in this masterpiece, and put them to work for you, you will be pleasantly surprised with the wonderful outcomes you can achieve.*"

Peggy McColl
New York Times Best-Selling Author

"I meet thousands of individuals each year who are committed to serving, to sharing, to enriching, and to inspiring others through their words, their actions, and their intentions.

When I first met Wrenwyck, I was impressed by his passion to serve. As I got to know him even more through the trainings and conversations, I realized that he is a leader among people. Wrenwyck is a man on a mission to do great things through his love, his compassion, and his commitment to those he meets and has the opportunity to lead. A true leader in every sense of the word, Wrenwyck is a shining example of what is good and strong and possible in each of us. Listen to him, follow his guidance, and reap the rewards of an extraordinary life for yourself and those around you."

Alice Haemmerle
Master NLP Trainer
Sydney, Australia 2012

"Wrenwyck Williams has taken a very complex topic and broken it down into small pieces so we can better understand the true meaning of our inspirational needs. I would highly recommend this book to anyone in pursuit of spiritual growth."

Don Cameron
Former President, Guilford Technical Community College

"I believe that there are unique people born in every generation who are catalysts for great change in the culture. Wrenwyck is one of those individuals. As you read this book, you will see and feel his passion to give hope and words of encouragement to anyone who desires to be more than the status quo. His thoughtful insights from his personal life experiences and life of faith will compel you to "GET UP" and do something great. This book will change your life."

Rev. James C. Hash, Jr.
Assistant Pastor, St. Peter's Church and World Outreach Center

"This book has already begun to change my life, and it will change the lives of all its readers. Wrenwyck's sage words resonate within the spirit and will unlock potential that many of us do not realize we already possess. Whether you are where you want to be in life or are lost and have unanswered questions, "Baby Food" is a blessing that we all should have in our toolbox of spiritual guidance."

Claudia Cano
Owner, Copy Editor & Proofreader
The Word Stylist

Baby Food

digestible concepts

Book 1: Faith

God said yes.... you said no.

by Wrenwyck Williams

© 2012 Wrenwyck Williams

All rights reserved. No part of this book may be reproduced or transmitted in any form or by any means, electronic or mechanical, including photocopying, recording, or by any information storage and retrieval system, without written permission of the publisher.

ISBN - 13: 978-0-9885203-0-1

Printed in the United States of America
Signature Book Printing, www.sbpbooks.com

*This book is not designed to, and does not, provide medical advice. All content ("content"), including text, graphics, images and information available on or through this book are for general informational purposes only.

The content is not intended to be a substitute for professional medical advice, diagnosis or treatment. Never disregard professional medical advice, or delay in seeking it, because of something you have read in this book. Never rely on information in this book in place of seeking professional medical advice.

Wrenwyck Williams nor Triune are responsible or liable for any advice, course of treatment, diagnosis or any other information that you obtain through this book. You are encouraged to confer with your doctor with regard to information contained on or through this book.

www.babyfoodbook.net

"Nothing that is True is New"

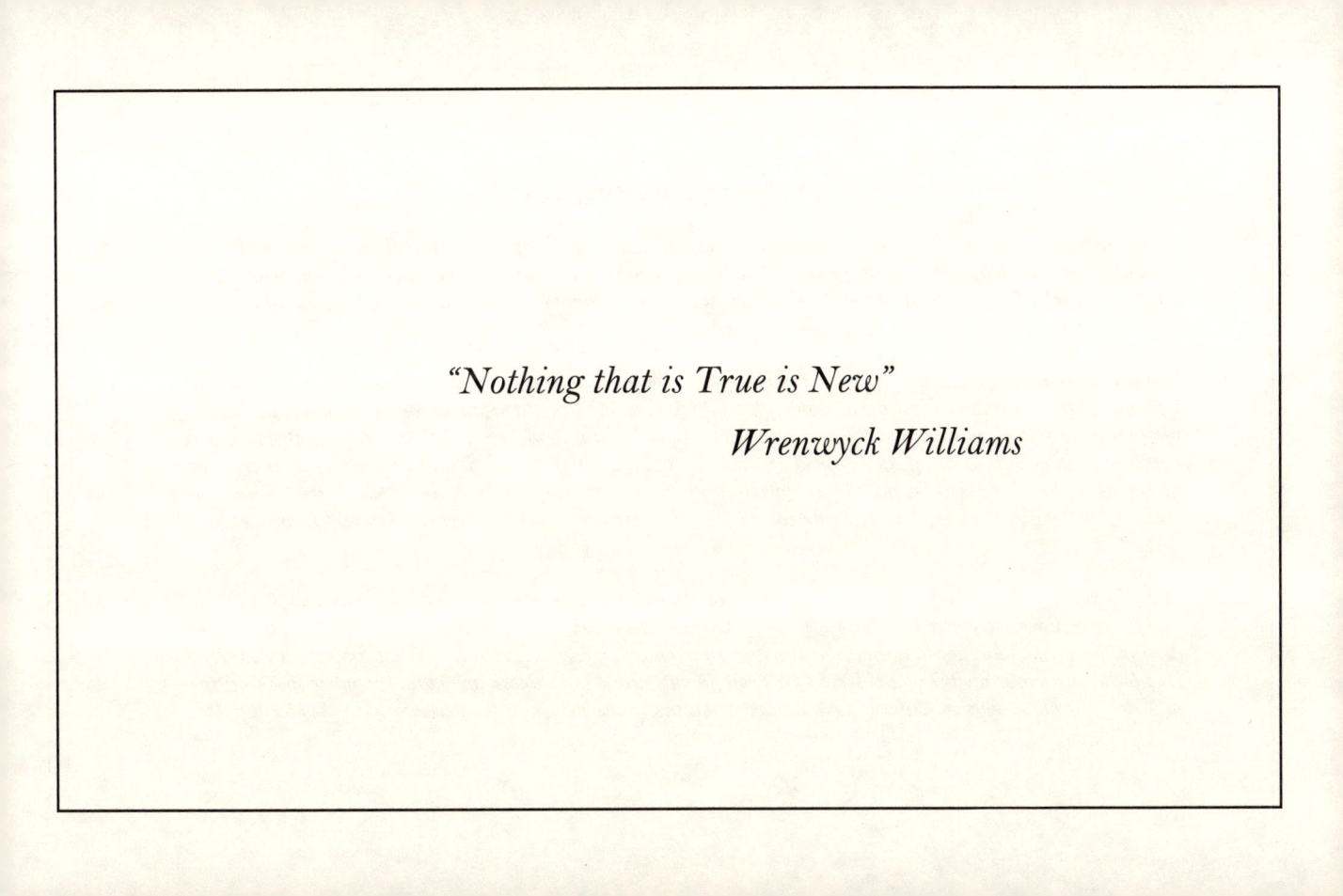

                                                  Wrenwyck Williams

Acknowledgements

God shared the concept for this book with me more than 13 years ago. I vividly remember the excitement I experienced at the thought of writing a book that could prove to be a catalyst for empowerment and growth for all. I was humbled and, to some extent, taken aback at the notion that God would use me to be the mailman in delivering what I knew would be revelation knowledge.

The ironic piece was that, after God shared this with me, for years I never heard him say anything else about it. I wondered if maybe it was just my own thought and not God speaking to me at all, or maybe God had found someone more suitable to carry out this task. No sooner than I had resigned myself to the fact that this task was not for me did he remind me of this book. This time, God was a bit more specific, which gave me more certainty that, indeed, this vision was for me. He would repeat this process over and over again. Each occurrence was more specific and detailed than the last. I wondered at times, "Why doesn't God just give it all to me? Why does he delay?"

Over the years, as I matured both spiritually and professionally, I came to understand that it was not God who was the impediment to getting the book written. It was me. Although not cognizant of it at the time, somewhere deep inside of me I did not feel worthy or capable. You know, you can only connect the dots going backward. As I looked back over my life and observed the professional success in business, accolades for public speaking, the ministerial achievements in winning souls and contributing to the body, and the development in leadership, I see now that God was doing all the things necessary to build the confidence, expertise, and faith needed for me to accept this commission. I began to realize that maybe, just maybe, I was good enough after all. Now that the maybes have turned to certainty, God, through the Holy Ghost, has inspired me to transcribe the message that he has in this book. Although I am still extremely humbled to be used in this manner, I am confident in my role as the mailman and convinced of the fact that this book is a large piece of my contribution to the world. I pray that reading this book will have as profound an effect on your life as it has had on mine in writing it. It was commissioned by God and inspired by the Holy Spirit. He calls it **Baby Food**.

I believe that there is no such thing as a self-made anything. Whatever success we experience in our lives can be contributed to someone and, in most cases, many people. In writing this book and having this project come to fruition, I offer my utmost gratitude to the following individuals.

The Holy Spirit for your inspiration and impartation. You and I know the truth.

To the greatest parents on earth, Samuel and Lucille Williams. You were such an awesome example for me and provided me with a childhood that most kids dream of. Thank you so much for the many sacrifices that you all made to ensure that we had the things that we needed and also wanted. It was you that I most admired and who has had the greatest impact on my life. Pop, you showed me what it meant to really be a husband and father and not merely a man. Most of all, I always knew I was loved and that my opinion always mattered. You introduced me to Jesus and lived a life before me that was consistent with his teaching. I love you very much and can never do enough to thank you, but I will certainly try.

To Wanda, the first real love of my life. You recognized potential in me at 19 that I did not know was there. Your encouragement, and love, in spite of myself, proved to be the essential ingredients in self-discovery for me. You have persevered through so much, I love you and am eternally grateful.

To my lovely daughters, Natasha and Naomi. You had me long before hello. You had me at conception. You are my joy, and I love you with everything within me. No father has ever been blessed with more beautiful, intelligent, and caring daughters. You have blessed my life more than you will ever know. I am so proud of both of you. As mentioned many times before, I have held many titles in my life, however the one that I am most proud of is "Daddy." "Let's floop this coop." (inside joke)

To my loving sisters and brother, Yvonne, Regina, and Stanwyck. I have so many wonderful memories of us growing up together. We did the things that most siblings do and some things that only we did. God has truly blessed me to be surrounded by siblings like each of you. I love you more than I can ever express. BTW, I just wanted you to know that I found out a long time ago that I wasn't really adopted. (smile)

To Bishop James C. Hash, Lady Joyce Hash, and my entire St. Peter's family. I cannot begin to express the gratitude that I have for all of you. Your mentoring and expressions of love and Godly example have provided me with a track to run on and a leader to look up to. I love you and thank you.

To Linah Tjung, you epitomize what true friendship is all about. You have supported me in every endeavor that I have undertaken, and you have richly enhanced my life. You have been a stalwart foundation in undergirding this project. Your persistent encouragement, can-do attitude, and remarkable insight have proved to be invaluable to me. It is rare that one meets an individual with such business savvy and an exceptional emotional quotient. I love you and am honored to call you my dear friend.

To Matt Lucas, you believed in me when **Baby Food** was only a title in mind, a belief expressed by your purchase of this book 10 years before one drop of ink was on the page. Thank you.

To Sam Pitts, for telling me over and over that the world was waiting for me. Sam, my friend, persistence does pay off. Thank you, and I love you.

Thanks to Alice Haemmerle and the entire Coaching Institute family, You have had a definite impact on my life, and I am so grateful. It is very good.

Kim Thorbourne, you are the best photographer on the planet. I am indebted to you.

To Mrs. Boykin, my 11th grade English teacher. You always said that I would be a poet or a writer. Thank you for making me stand and recite all of those poems in class. You would be proud to know that I have won over 40 speech contests and am a Toastmasters International-DTM. You were the hardest teacher that I ever had, and I love you for it.

Commission

To enlighten God's people to who they truly are and to empower them with the authority that God has given them. To reveal the truth about faith both spiritually and scientifically. To share the methods that will enable them to fulfill their purposes and create the lives they were destined to have. In doing so, creating overflowing resources to sow into God's kingdom, to greatly glorify God, and prosper them!

"Commissioned by God, inspired by the Holy Spirit"

Baby Food

Table of Contents

I. Nothing That is True is New — 1

II. Who Are You? — 9

III. Coming Out of the Matrix — 24

IV. God Said Yes...You Said No — 29

V. Faith's House...The Subconscious Mind — 40

VI. Strong or Weak Faith...That is the Question — 49

VII. Keep Your Healing...Turn off the TV — 66

VIII. Above All, Prosper and Be in Good Health — 83

Nothing That is True is New

Why do we struggle and experience poor health in a world that was created for us in which to prosper and be healthy? Why is it that, even though we have unlimited power, do we accept a mediocre and, many times, unfulfilled life? Why, when our tongues and heart can move mountains, do we use them primarily to feel despair and to speak about our lack of resources? Do you wonder why it is that some seem to be so richly blessed while others seem to struggle generation after generation? Why it is that some seem to have happiness, great health, and a life of bliss, while others seem to be up and down and, unfortunately, experience one cold or illness after another?

What if you could do, have, and be whatever you choose? What if there were no stipulations or limitations on you to give in abundance to the people you love or to the causes you support? What if it was revealed that concealed inside you lies the combination to unlock a world that you could uniquely create, a world full of an abundance of joy, peace, resources, and love?

Wouldn't that be worth pursuing?

Well, not only is it possible, it is actually quite probable. In fact, you should be creating the life that you desire for yourself and your loved ones daily. You should be enjoying great health and prosperity and living daily in a constant state of gratitude. You have been endowed with the power to have anything that you focus strong thought on to be able to come to fruition in your life. The unfortunate thing is that most of you either do not know it or you know it but do not believe it. Either way, this incomparable power has been negated in your life. It is like asking what the difference is between a person who cannot read and one who doesn't read. Exactly. Unfortunately, they are both ignorant.

Like me, many of you have been long-time subscribers of the concepts explained in great books like the Law of Attraction, The Blessing of Abraham, and the movie The Secret. I believe that these works are fantastic. However, I must say that in reality these concepts and teachings are not secrets at all. The truth has been available to us for thousands of years. It is only a revelation to us if we were not aware of its existence or if we misunderstood its meaning. Well, I can sum it up for you in two simple scriptures. According to your faith, be it on to you, and as a man thinketh so is he...PERIOD. However, the key is how you effectively apply these scriptures to your everyday life and, as a result, create the life that you desire.

The process to make the aforementioned things a reality in your life is derived from one somewhat misunderstood concept. This concept is called faith. It is infallible and will 100% of the time bring to you the things that you 100% believe that you already have. It has no stipulations, is not biased by race, creed, color, religion, or, dare I say, even the will of our loving God. Careful here. I didn't say that it is not profitable to pray God's will. I am saying that your receiving of the requests that you desire or not receiving it is not predicated on God wanting you to have it. Trust me, God could care less about what kind of car you drive.

The term faith is generally familiar to most. However, only a few ever really utilize it to its fullest extent and, as a result, are resigned to live a life of mediocrity and lack.

After reading this book, you will gain a thorough understanding of what faith truly is and how to effectively use it. It will be revealed to you that faith actually is not a concept at all but a tangible entity of unlimited power. It will be explained to you in no uncertain terms exactly how faith works both spiritually and scientifically. Once you have fully digested these concepts, you will no longer have an excuse for not attaining the prosperous life that God has prepared for you. You will no longer be able to use God and "His will" as a scapegoat for generations of poverty and illness. Most of all, you will be enlightened as to who and what you really are and, as a result, will expect and ultimately aspire to create great things in your life. In doing so, you will glorify God and bring prosperity to your life. ARE YOU READY?

If you are nodding to yourself right now as an affirmative indication, then it is time for you to see what is on the following pages of this book. As a matter of fact, if you have been led to pick up this book at all, regardless of how you were made aware of its existence, it is because you have an innate desire to have more, to see more, to be more, and to give more.

Let's begin this journey by examining the common perception of the average Christian. Take a moment, and draw a mental picture of what you feel a Christian looks like. Go ahead. I'll wait. What did you see? More than likely you probably saw a very mediocre-looking somebody. Well, Wrenwyck, what's wrong with mediocre? Nothing, except I know that you and I were never created to be or live in this manner. With this as a perception, there is no wonder why the world is reluctant to come to Christ. God said that above all we should prosper and be in good health even as our soul prospers. Now I will expand on this a bit later. However, at this juncture I feel it is important to set a strong foundation for the basis of this book. Remember that we are to be ambassadors for Christ on Earth. As ambassadors, we are a representation of Him on this planet. It is no different than a person being an ambassador from the United States to Australia. Being an ambassador from the United States means that you are a representation of what our country is all about. Individuals in Australia should be able to observe you, your lifestyle, and even countenance and gain insight as to how the United States is. They should not have to travel to the United States when they can simply observe you, because you represent the country. Now, just what would they think about our country if you were living in a tent, riding a bicycle, and begging for food? What type of country must the United States be to have their ambassador living like this? One thing that I am sure they would not want to do is visit the United States. If this is how they care for their own, how would they treat foreigners? How are we representing God? Now, just pause and think for a moment. How is it that a father with unlimited resources could raise children who have not enough to eat? Is it God's fault that many are living below their means as his ambassadors, sons, and daughters? God has done all He can to ensure that we all have more than enough of everything. He has left it in His will and given us power of attorney so that we may have access to His estate at all times. We do not even have to complete any paperwork, credit checks, or provide stipulated tenure of employment. It is irrelevant as to what car, house, spouse, or lifestyle that you desire. It is all yours. Well, why do we not possess it? The truth is we have been misled, manipulated, malnourished, and misinformed for far too long. All too often when it comes to spiritual matters, we have only emphasized the sin aspects and, as a result, many adults are filled with **CONDEMNATION**, *which has made them feel unworthy and left them weak. No wonder* *many men do not like coming to church. Please do not misunderstand me here. I love church, and I know that there are many others that do as well. However, there are many that are sitting there just waiting to go home because each week they are made to feel that they serve a God who is mad at them and is just waiting to punish them for making mistakes...NOT TRUE. Just so you know, we serve a God that is full of LOVE and GRACE. Jesus went to the cross for all of the mistakes that you will ever make. So, do not cast down your confidence. You are much more than you ever have imagined.*

There is a paradigm shift happening in the body of Christ even as you read this book. It is my commission from God to share information and concepts revealed to me by Him that will contribute to this great shift in thinking. It is time for us to be enlightened and empowered so that we may walk in the authority that was given to us. It is time for the body of Christ to take its rightful place in this world and for us to stop conforming to a life of passivity and mediocrity. We are not commissioned to merely create a life for ourselves but to make a profound difference. Aren't you tired of just attending church week after week with no significant changes in your life, church, and city? Well, if you feel a bit stagnant in the growth and impact that the body of Christ is having, how do you think God is feeling? Let's make a decision right now to stop just accepting whatever happens in our lives as others do and to make a mental transformation that will produce intended results and create supernatural living. Let's open our minds and understand that all we have been taught is not all there is to know. Let's begin today to truly understand and apply the power of faith in a manner that has not been witnessed since the days that our Lord and savior walked the streets of Nazareth. Trust me when I say that Jesus' words from John 14:12 still ring true today: "Verily, verily, I say unto you, He that believeth on me, the works that I do shall he do also; and Greater works than these shall he do." Do you believe it? Remember, according to your faith be it on to you, not according to God's faith.

- Digest this: (The power is in you. Stop waiting on God. He has done his part. He is waiting on you.)

Who are You?

Who are you anyway? What may be even more important is what are you? Let us start there. Let me begin by saying that you are a triune being (three in one). You are a spirit (energy), you possess a mind (soul, emotions), and your mode of expression and transportation is your body. Basically, you are a spirit being having a human experience. You are a specific agent on a specific mission. You have been endowed with a unique personality, physical traits, and abilities designed to be attributes to the success of your mission. Remember that the purpose always precedes the invention. You and your mission are a pertinent part of a master strategic plan designed and orchestrated by God long before you were ever born. Ephesians 1:11 states, "In whom also we have obtained an inheritance, being predestinated according to the purpose of him who works all things after the counsel of his own will."

That's right: You are on a mission. You play a vital role in the plan of the one who is all knowing, possesses all power, and is and will be forever present. This information alone should make you sit up just a bit straighter. Just think about how you feel when the CEO of your place of business calls you just by your name. You go back to your office or cubicle and you say to your peers, "Hey, Mr. Alexander said hello to me today. He actually knew what my name was." You are beside yourself with pride. You reckon that you must be doing some pretty good work if the big man knows you. Isn't this right? You walk even taller if you are in a position to be a part of your company's management team and actually play an integral part in determining the goals, direction, and strategy of the company. Oh man, and don't have your name on the outside of your office and a designated place to park. Shoot, you feel like you are already in heaven. If you feel important merely playing a role in your CEO's vision, how much more do you mean to this world when you are playing a role in the plan of Him who created your CEO? Your company, no matter where you work, can only take raw materials that are already here and make things that are useful. Maybe it is medicine, electronics, automobiles, or furniture. All of these things are fantastic, but they have to be comprised of the raw materials that this planet already produces. I am talking about being part of the plan of He who created the raw materials. Are you starting to see a bit of who you are?

Now that we have digested the fact that you are uniquely designed for the mission that you have, we must also understand how to properly use the tools that we have been given to succeed in this mission.

Remember when we stated that you are a triune being? We said that you possess a mind and live in your body. Saying that you (being a spirit) possess a mind and a body implies that this mind and body are slaves to you and, as a result, should be subjected to your authority. You should control and use them as if they were tools. You should be able to call upon them to do your bidding at any time, day or night. This is true, as it is with any living possession, as long as you have disciplined them. Think of it as owning a horse on a farm. The horse has the potential to do a variety of things that may be of great benefit to you on your farm. It can pull a plow, carry you to and from the market, or even provide riding for enjoyment on a sunny Saturday afternoon. It may have all of this potential. However, until it is tamed it will not be the useful animal that it should be. The same is true with your mind and your body. They should be under subjection to your spirit. Unfortunately, so many of us have not disciplined our minds and, as a result, it runs rabid around this planet doing whatever it chooses and, at times, does things that are detrimental to the precise functionality of the body. Let me give you an analogy that will provide a bit more insight. You have a car that you own, right? Well, just imagine that you are in the inside of the car, representing your spirit, and the car itself represents your body. You have an onboard computer that regulates everything. This computer should be operated and controlled by you based upon what lever or button you press. For example, if you want cruise control, you press the appropriate lever, and the computer in response tells the car to govern itself and maintain a certain speed. The car responds by doing precisely what the computer said. This computer represents your mind. All good, right? However, there are times when this computer malfunctions. Using the same analogy, you (spirit) want to cruise down the highway at 75. You press the appropriate cruise control levers and, to your surprise, the car goes up to 90. Wait a minute! What is this about? I want to go 75. You go through the same procedure, and again your car (body) controlled by the computer (mind) goes 90. It is as if it has a mind of its own. It is mocking you. You (spirit) know what the speed limit is, and you (spirit) have every intention of obeying it. However, your onboard computer (mind), which controls your car (body), is not cooperating with you. Now, because you have been distracted by this undisciplined, unruly behavior, the next thing that you notice are blue lights flashing behind you, and the officer does not look happy. Your mind has caused your body to do things that are detrimental to you. Are you getting this? This is in total opposition to the way the manufacturer intended for this car to function. Now, when you are in your car and the onboard computer is functioning properly, you can perform whatever function you like. You can put the top up or down, adjust the radio, control the windshield wipers, input the appropriate information in your navigation system, and literally create what atmosphere you would like in your transportation world. To help you in facilitating these functions, the manufacturer has given you an owner's manual. So it is with us. Our spirits, the real us, should be in control and ensure that our minds are disciplined and under subjection to us. As a result, our bodies will follow. This is vitally important to creating success in our lives and the fulfillment of our mission. Like the automobile manufacturer, our manufacturer has also given us an owner's manual. It is called the Bible. Are you following me? Well, why is it that our minds do not just fall in line as they should? Why does this onboard computer have the capacity to make decisions that are contrary to what we would desire? The reason is that God loves us so much that he has given us free will. Although he wishes that we all obey and be saved, he does not mandate it. It would be like forcing your mate to love you. Who wants love like that? In fact, in that scenario, it would not be love at all.

With this free will to choose yes or no at times, it can create a bit of disarray. It would be synonymous with a game of chess. Get a mental picture of God playing chess. He has his twelve pieces all with a variety of different attributes. He has Pawns and Knights that can move in the shape of an "L" and Rooks that can move from side to side and up and down. He has Bishops who can move all the way across the board diagonally and, of course, he has the all-powerful Queen and King. All the pieces have their role, and their abilities are tied to the specific role that they have. At the very beginning of the game, God has already orchestrated a master plan that will ultimately create a winning strategy for the entire team. Before the first move is made, the game has mentally already been won. There are no worries as long as all the pieces are working in concert with one another and are willing to be moved and even sacrificed if necessary by the chess player. However, as mentioned earlier, we have free will, and, at times, we that are Knights want to be Rooks, and the Rooks want to be Queens and so on. This is where we sometimes find our lives to be challenging and unfulfilled. We are attempting to play a role or live a life that is not in alignment with the purpose or qualities that we possess. You are not seeing the true genius of who you are because you are attempting to operate in a role that was not created for you. This is why it is necessary to renew your mind. In doing this we will prove what is the good, the acceptable, and perfect will of God. Part of this perfect will is to live a life that is reminiscent of God.

Now, how do we create the lifestyle we desire and fulfill the purpose for which we are here? Very simply, we create it through our thoughts. With our thoughts we can create any atmosphere or lifestyle we choose. However, we must not allow our minds to just aimlessly think of things that are not in line with our intended purpose. Unintentional thoughts will bring unintended results. Disciplined, intentional thoughts will bring intended results. Please understand that thoughts are things. They are real and tangible, just like seeds that are planted in a garden. If you plant green pea seeds, fertilize, and water them, then in time you will have green peas. If you plant butterbeans, fertilize, and water them, then, in time, you will have butterbeans. If you just grab a bunch of seeds not knowing of what sort, fertilize, and water them, then, in time, you have no idea what type of harvest you will have. So it is with your thoughts. What you think about you bring about. Thoughts are things (seeds). Even though we cannot see them with our natural eyes, I can assure you that in time we will certainly see the results of these thoughts, whether intentional or unintentional. The key obviously is how to make sure that we are thinking intentional thoughts and how to create the future we desire. Once again, I would state that you have probably read many books and attended many seminars that explain the process of setting goals, writing them down, and taking massive action. In addition, you have been exposed to the profitable nature of speaking positive things consistently to override, if not replace, the negative unintentional thoughts all together. As mentioned earlier in this book, nothing that is true is new. If you simply go back to the Bible in Habakka 2:2 it states, *"And the LORD answered me, and said, write the vision, and make it plain upon tables, so he may run that reads it."* It goes on to state in Joshua 1:8, *"This book of the law shall not depart out of thy mouth; but thou shalt meditate therein day and night, that thou mayest observe to do according to all that is written therein: for then thou shalt make thy way prosperous, and then thou shalt have good success."* Notice here that it is the process that I am more importantly attempting to get you to grasp. We know how important the laws of Moses were at the time and still are today. However, we also know that Jesus arrived, and now we live under the law of the spirit of life. The process was to write the vision down and make it plain. What we need to take from this is how important it is to be specific. Next, we must read the vision so that we can take massive action or run with it. It MUST penetrate your subconscious mind. Then, remember what we spoke about earlier. What you think about you bring about. In Joshua, we see the importance of meditating or thinking on the word of God day and night. As a matter of fact, the Bible states to not let the words depart from your mouth. This means that you should always be thinking about and speaking about it. Now you have a goal. You have written it down so you can clearly see it and are specific about it. Next, *to ensure that your thought life is in line with what your goal is, you are thinking and speaking on God's word day and night. Please understand that your mind will always give precedence to what you are saying over what you are thinking. So if you are thinking negative thoughts and getting negative or unwanted results, you had better start speaking, and I mean right now! Just in case this mind process is foreign to you, take a moment and take this simple test. Keep in mind that what we are proving is the fact that your mind will give precedence to what you are saying over what you are thinking. It will not process both at the same time. Now, I want you to close your eyes and begin to mentally recite your ABCs to yourself (not out loud). When you get to the letter K, I want you to start counting out loud from 1 to 10. Are you ready? Okay, start reciting your ABCs in your head. If you did the exercise, when you got to the letter K and began to count to 10 out loud, what happened to the ABCs? Exactly. They were erased from your mind, and you concentrated only on the counting. This is why it is so important to speak things out loud. If you do this on a consistent basis, everything that you are saying will become the dominant thoughts that you will be thinking. When those become your intentional thoughts, then you will get your intended results. This process will enable you to make an impression on your subconscious mind. Once it has penetrated this entity, your thoughts will become a reality and manifest themselves with 100% accuracy and consistency. You must learn to focus and think on purpose. Remember, the scripture also says that you should confess with your mouth and believe in your heart. Jesus goes on to state in Mark 11:23, "For verily I say unto you, That whosoever shall say unto this mountain, Be thou removed, and be thou cast into the sea; and shall not doubt in his heart, but shall believe that those things which he saith shall come to pass; he shall have whatsoever he saith." What you repeatedly hear you will inevitably believe. Are you following me? Now, the fertilization and watering process of our thoughts is our continued affirmative confession that we already have those things about which we are thinking. Keep focusing, and apply the appropriate action. Remember, faith without works is dead. You may be thinking, "Wrenwyck, how do you know it works?" You are reading this book...aren't you? (smile)*

Now that we understand that we are triune beings, how is it that we are able to have our thoughts create whatever it is that we would like to see? How is it that, just by imagining with strong focus followed by specific action, we can actually create our own paradise? Put your seatbelts on for this one.

I am sure that we all can agree that everything reproduces after its own kind. Orange seeds will give you only oranges. Apple seeds will give you only apples. Two dogs mating will never produce a cat. Are you following me? Well, based on the Holy Bible (scripture), God has created us in His own image and likeness. In addition, the Bible states that He breathed the breath of life in us. Where did God get this breath? Exactly. It was His own. So He breathed His own spirit into us. Let's look at this a bit closer. Based on Dictionary.com, image is defined as a physical likeness or representation of a person, animal, or thing that is photographed, painted, sculpted, or otherwise made visible. Likeness is defined as the condition of being alike, to the same degree, equally. With this as our reference, we can see once again that everything including God produces after its own kind.

So here we go. Are you ready? If God is God, and He created us in His own image and likeness and breathed His breath in to us, how is it that we, too, are not a god? It is not possible. You are not God, but you are a god. No, this is not blasphemy. It is blasphemy to refute or deny the power that is in you. Did Jesus not say in John 10:31-34 "31Then the Jews took up stones again to stone him. 32Jesus answered them, Many good works have I showed you from my Father; for which of those works do ye stone me? 33The Jews answered him, saying, For a good work we stone thee not; but for blasphemy; and because that thou, being a man, makest thyself God. 34Jesus answered them, Is it not written in your law, I said, Ye are gods?" So here we can see that Jesus clearly states that we, too, are gods. Once again, not God but a god. We are from the same source. Let me give you an example. Let's say you have a large pitcher of water and a small empty cup. Now, you pour water from the pitcher into the cup, filling it up. The cup is full from the water that was contained in the pitcher. Is there any difference in the water in the small cup and the water that was in the pitcher? Obviously, the answer is no. In the same vein, God poured himself into our dirt bodies. The same spirit, the same God. There is no other. We, just as God, can create in our own image and likeness. We, just as God, can speak things into being just as He has. He said, "Let there be light," and there was light. Jesus said, "If ye had faith as a grain of mustard seed, ye might say unto this sycamore tree, Be thou plucked up by the root, and be thou planted in the sea; and it should obey you." Here, you see Jesus exclaiming that we can speak things into being and into not being just as God did. The key here is IF you have the faith.

Now, we understand who we are and why it is that we, too, are capable of using faith to change our circumstances and make a difference in this world. God has given us all the measure of faith with which we can and should use to fulfill the purposes for which we are here. But how?

How do we really use this awesome force? For you Star Wars *fans, you will find great parallels in the Force used in the movie and faith in your life. Just as they would differentiate in the movie that Luke Skywalker was strong in the Force while others were not so strong, we, too, have different degrees of strength in faith. Although, as stated, we were all given the measure of faith. The question is what did you do with the measure that was given to you?*

- *Digest this: (God created you in his image and likeness. As God is, so you are. Accept this and be accountable for the power that God has endowed you with. Just as God did, you likewise should speak your world into being, in doing so, creating success for yourself, glorifying God, and making a profound difference in this world.)*

Coming out of the Matrix

"Be ye not conformed but ye transformed by the renewing of your mind." Romans 12:2
Consider for just a moment classic movies like The Wizard of Oz, The Matrix, *and* Star Wars. *What are the almost mirror-like similarities in each movie? The star character in each is just an ordinary person. They meet a wizard of sorts and then experience excitement and enlightenment. In* Star Wars, *for Luke Skywalker it was Yoda who enlightened him. In* The Wizard of Oz, *it was the Wizard who enlightened Dorothy, and in* The Matrix *it was Morpheus who enlightened Neo. Isn't it amazing that once all three were enlightened and gained insight to who they really were, a whole new world opened up for them? Neo, because of this insight, refused to conform to the ordinary and powerless world of the Matrix. He transformed (changed in nature, form, character, or condition; metamorphosed) and accepted that he was The One, and this acknowledgement revealed the powers to overcome his circumstances that were there all along. Dorothy then realized, as well as her traveling companions, that whatever each was seeking, they actually already had. In* Star Wars, *once*

Luke understood that he was very strong in the Force, he was able to use it to ultimately defeat Darth Vader and the dark side and bring peace and reconciliation to his family. It is no coincidence that all three movies were the top-grossing films of their time. Why is it that we seem to flock to the theaters to view movies of this type? Is it just because we love adventure? Is it because somewhere innate within us we recognize that it really isn't make believe at all? These stories resonate with us because innately there is something that says, "I, too, am Neo." In Romans 12:2, it states, "To be ye not conformed, but be ye transformed by the renewing of your mind. That ye may prove what is the good, the acceptable, and perfect will of God." Maybe it's just me, but I want to prove His perfect will. I want to glorify God in such a mighty way that people will run, fly, swim, and sail from all over the world just to hear of His love and mighty works. I want to have walk-on-water faith. Don't you? Does this frighten you? Or maybe you're thinking that was just for Jesus and Peter. Really? I beg to differ. Peter was just the only one bold enough to believe that, "If Jesus said so, then I can do it." Hey, understand something. It was not Jesus' faith that enabled Peter to walk on water. It was Peter's. It was Jesus' word that ignited Peter's faith. Jesus said "I am the same yesterday, today and forever more." He is not preventing us now. We merely have not renewed our minds to the extent that we accept it as being possible. When we do, WE WILL WALK! It's okay. In the movies mentioned earlier, all the characters felt the same way. They felt that they were not equal to the tasks that were placed before them. They were bound by their limited thinking, dependent upon their natural abilities, and enslaved in the matrix in which they lived. They all had to renew their minds, which transformed them from natural to supernatural. What is the difference between Peter and you? Have you actually seen Jesus? Have you walked and eaten with Him and still denied Him three times? Were you rebuked because of your misguided sayings? Yet this man who did all these things walked on the water. You have not denied Him three times, have you? Why don't we walk? Remember that Jesus said on many occasions that it is your faith that has healed you. In each account, it was action taking place that activated their faith. In this case, the mere fact that Peter asked is evidence that he believed that Jesus' word would make it possible. If Peter had felt that it was impossible for him, then he never would have asked. Please note the wisdom of Jesus here. His response to Peter was simply, "Come." He did not say if you feel like it is possible for you. I believe that had He said that, Peter would have still been in the boat today. When Jesus said "Come," Peter by himself climbed out of the boat and walked on the water. Peter simply acted on what he believed to be true, which was Jesus' word. Peter's faith enabled him to walk based on Jesus' word. It was not Jesus' faith but Peter's. The power is in you. According to YOUR faith, be it on to you! This is also evident by Jesus stating that in His hometown, He marveled at the lack of faith of its residents. Due to this lack of faith, He COULD NOT do any mighty works, except heal a few. Notice that He did not say that He WOULD NOT. That would imply that it was possible, but He chose not to do it. He said He COULD NOT. The reason that He said He could not was due to THEIR lack of faith, not His own. Are you following me? Peter walked on the water because of his faith, not Jesus'. It is time that we stop passing the buck and waiting for God to do everything. He endowed us with POWER from on high and gave us His wonderful son as a Savior and example. Let's stop repeating the same limiting messages over and over again and renew our minds to the *unlimited potential that we have based on His word. Let's not merely have potential. Let's fulfill our potential. We, too, are Neo, and the world is waiting on us!*

- *Digest this: (You will never succeed past your ability to see yourself as successful. You will never be greater than the thoughts that you have about yourself. Please know that you, too, are Neo, if you can believe that you are.)*

God Said Yes...You Said No

Okay, buckle up! Now that we have generated a bit of momentum by examining who you really are, and in essence, why this infallible force can and will work for you, let's continue to ascend into another dimension. This dimension generally is not fully understood, but nonetheless its results are unquestionably evident and undeniably consistent. Now, let's define, examine, and uncover the truth about FAITH. Let me begin by sharing a story with you.

When I was about 8 or 9 years old, my family lived in Kaiserslautern, Germany. My parents always raised us to believe in God and to pray every night. Well, on this particular Saturday afternoon one of my friends, Steve Berlin, and I went to the movies. It was cool because back then you could see the matinee for a quarter and the next movie for just 35 cents. The popcorn was 15 cents for plain and 20 cents for buttered. For whatever reason, I forgot my popcorn money. I asked Steve several times for 20 cents, but each time I asked, he said no, he needed it. At this point, all I wanted to do was punch him right in the dag gone nose, but I didn't because I was still hoping he would change his mind. That's when it hit me that I could pray. I remembered the scripture that stated, "Ask and you shall receive." I received that scripture literally as an eight year old, and I remember the joy that I felt when I remembered it. At that age, I did not understand that the Holy Ghost would bring these things to your remembrance. I was so happy and totally convinced that I would be tasting that buttered popcorn soon. I looked at Steve with a renewed spirit and asked, "Steve, may I have 20 cents to get some buttered popcorn?" Without hesitation, he reached in his pocket, handed me the money, and never said one word. I said quietly to myself "Thank you, God. It works. It works." Little did I know that God had not even shown himself yet. As I spun out of my chair and began the glorious walk up the aisle to the concession stand, a very old woman was sitting on the end of the row. She appeared to me to be at least 100. She never looked at me. However, as I approached her chair she simply reached out and handed me a bag of buttered popcorn. I was awestruck as I thanked her and turned around and walked slowly back to my seat. I never got to the concession stand at all. God is so good and so real. This was my first encounter with the awesome power *of faith. It was a process that I would repeat over and over again, even as I write this book. I must admit that I never gave Steve back the twenty cents that he gave me. Somehow I reasoned within myself that, since he had made me ask so many times, I deserved it. Plus, God must have wanted me to have it (remember, I was very young).*

The point here is that it is in the acting with 100% certainty that we receive from God, through the power of faith. If I had not asked again with conviction, I would not have received the money. If I had not received the money, I would have never walked up the aisle and received the popcorn from someone I am 100% convinced was a spirit. Yes, I said spirit. They do exist, and this one was in the form of an elderly woman.

Now, I want to share this right up front so that we may continue to ascend. The ONLY thing that moves the hand of God is our FAITH. That is all that has ever moved Him and all that ever will. Not our tears, not our sacrifices, not our moaning, begging, or even our prayers where no faith is involved. Only true faith will activate the hand of God and in doing so will give us access to all His unlimited resources. Notice I use the word activate here. Dictionary. com defines activate as to make active, cause to function, or act. This is important because that is precisely what happens when you use faith. Your faith causes God to become active in your situation and bring about the results that you desire 100% of the time. If that is so, Wrenwyck, then why is it that so many do not receive from God what they are desiring? I'm glad that you asked.

First, let's define faith. Many believe that having strong belief in wanting or not wanting something (like illness) is faith. Well, this is close but not totally accurate.

Faith IS NOT belief, although belief is certainly a part of the equation. Faith is not a sole act at all but a process. Faith is the process of acting on what you are totally convinced that you already have. True faith is not activated until that second that you are totally convinced. This 100% assurance compels action and simultaneously activates the hand of God. Belief alone will not move mountains, but certainly acting on what you are totally convinced that you already have will. In saying this, we understand that this thing that you are totally convinced of remains, at the instant, unseen to the natural eye. Otherwise, you would not need faith. Are you with me? Let me also state that the strength of your faith (the extent of your conviction or certainty) will determine the timeliness of this process.

In the story I shared to begin this chapter, even though I was not aware of this faith process, I executed it precisely and, as a result, received what I was desiring for. First, I desired to have the buttered popcorn. I believed when I prayed that, with 100% certainty, I already had it. This certainty that I possessed compelled me to act. I asked again for the 20 cents to purchase the popcorn. My action was based on my total conviction that I would receive, and it released my faith and activated the hand of God. I ended up with the popcorn and the 20 cents.

In Hebrews 11:1 it states that, "Now, Faith is the substance of things hoped for the evidence of things not seen." In verse 6 it states that, "But without faith it is impossible to please him; for he that cometh to God must believe that he is and that he is a rewarder of them that diligently seek him." Let's look at this a bit closer. The key words here are Now, Hope, Substance, and Evidence. For many years, I believed that faith was acting on what you believed and having great expectation of receiving it. I understand now that it is not. It is the process of acting on what you believe once you are totally convinced that you already have it. The reason I state that it is once you are totally convinced that you already have it is because many people act in hope and not total conviction. Basically, they are merely trying it in hopes that it works. This is why many do not receive from God. It is only action out of total certainty that will activate the hand of God and give you access to His unlimited resources. *(WRITE THIS DOWN, PLEASE. IT IS MAJOR.)* You may act in a manner that is consistent to what you are hoping for, and that is not all bad because this action may, in time, develop in total conviction. However, please understand that it is in that precise moment that, when you are 100% convinced that you already have it, the action will instantaneously activate the hand of God. It is like placing a pot of water on the stove with an objective of getting it to boil and create steam. You place it on the stove and turn the dial to the high position. If you stand there and watch it, you will see the water start to move around and even bubble a bit. However, until that water gets to 212 degrees Fahrenheit, it will not boil, and no steam will be produced. Are you following me?

There is the word NOW preceding faith in this scripture. If it is not Now, it is not faith. I have noticed that some Bible translations have taken the word Now out. Please put it back in. This is the key. It is either Now Faith or No Faith. Our God is a Now God only. With God, it is always right now. We tend to take some time to get ourselves in a place where we are totally convinced. Our true faith is then released, and right then the hand of God is activated.

Let me give you an example. We all know that Abraham was considered the father of faith. God had promised Abraham when he was 75 that he would have many descendants of his own flesh. However, Abraham did not have Isaac until he was 100 years old. What took so long? Was it God? Many think this was the case, but I contend that it was not. I believe that God could not move and make this come to pass until Abraham and Sarah had developed *their faith to the extent that they were totally convinced that what God had promised they had already received. They obviously were acting in an attempt to become pregnant, but they were acting in hope. We know that they were not certain because Sarah laughed at the thought of even conceiving a child at their advanced age. God had to help Abraham by changing his name and showing him all the stars in the sky and the grains of sand on the beach. He had to get Abraham to see this image clearly so that he could become totally convinced. Once he had this conviction without any doubt, Isaac was conceived. Abraham was 100 years old. The 25-year lapse in time was not God delaying but in Abraham acting on what he was totally convinced that he already had.*

The scripture then says substance, meaning the real physical matter of which a person or thing consists, as in "DNA is the substance of our genes." As you know, this DNA will accurately identify who we are in relation to the other 7 billion people on the planet. So it is with your faith. It will accurately identify exactly what it is that you are 100% convinced that you have already received. In saying this, I feel it is necessary to state that hope is a necessary piece of the equation as well. Without hope, you have nothing for your faith to be the substance of. Here is a nugget for you: "Without hope, faith has no purpose." (Bishop James C. Hash, St. Peter's Church and World Outreach Center)

Next, we know that Now Faith is also the evidence of things unseen. It's like having direct deposit from your place of employment. Typically, when this is the case you don't actually receive a check that can be cashed. Instead, you get a stub, a statement if you will, that indicates how much you actually made and how much was deposited in your designated account. That stub becomes the evidence that you have been compensated and that the funds have been deposited and are available to be used. Based on this alone, you ACT (as though you have already received it. You are 100% convinced that you have the funds). You get off of work and take your family out to eat, purchase gas on the way, and even have bills scheduled to be paid out of this account, without ever physically seeing a dime. Wow! You really have faith in your employer! In this same fashion, your faith becomes the evidence of things that you hope for but have not actually seen. You don't have to see it because you have FAITH. Now, all you have to do is act on whatever it is that you are hoping for and are convinced that you have already received. Your employer shared with you that your compensation was in your account and gave you a piece of paper to prove it. God said in Mark 11:24 that "Whatsoever things that you desire, when you pray believe that you receive it, and you shall have it." He went on to say that, "According to your faith, be it on to you." I do not know how much clearer He could be. Now, whose word do you think we should more assuredly act on? Your employer's or God's? We all know the right answer. However, more times than not we tend to trust our sight or some physical evidence over God, even though the word says that we walk by faith, not by sight. You know, when you think about it, we always seem to trust the things or people we know the best. Are you following me? The closer our relationship with God and His word, the more faith we develop and confidence that His word is true. Faith comes by hearing and hearing by the word of God. Before we move on from this topic, I want to reiterate that in Mathew 9:29, Jesus states, "According to your faith be it on to you." There is no stipulation here. In Mark 11:24, He says "Whatsoever you desire," not if God wants you to have it or if He feels you are ready for it. According to your faith, be it on to you, that is it. I will say however, that you pray in vain if you pray for things that are contrary to His word. For example, I cannot pray for someone's child to be injured so that my daughter can be the cheerleading captain. You with me? God does not care that you have things. Please understand that. He just doesn't want things to have you. I think we should have a good understanding that Now Faith is the process of acting on what you are totally convinced that you already have. This is what activates the hand of God. You got it?

- *Digest this: (Every answer to your petition prayer that is not contrary to God's word is "Yes!" If you do not receive your requested desire, it is not God. It is you.)*

- *Please understand that you have to "Saw it before you See it." Wrenwyck Williams*

Faith's House...The Subconscious Mind

I believe that this spiritually unlimited force (FAITH) is the component that we possess that makes us like God. I also believe that it resides in the subconscious mind. As discussed earlier, God made us in His image and likeness. This is vitally important because it clearly explains why you can and should be living a victorious life. Have you ever noticed that many of the motivational speakers have conducted seminar after seminar and produced CDs and DVDs on what techniques you should use to bring you wealth and prosperity, and yet only 5% of the people in the world are truly wealthy? The reason is that most people really do not believe that these techniques will work for them, even though collectively they spend billions each year. I am not knocking them, but the motivational speakers also know that most people will not achieve the things they talk about. It is not their fault because the techniques they share do work. It is the individual who usually, and subconsciously, believes that they are not the right type and, because of these defeated beliefs, generally give up. They are merely attempting it. They have no real substantiation that they can do it. They have the proof that it can be done, but nothing to substantiate that they can do it. They have no evidence to support the belief that it will work for them. For example, what would make a dog think that it could roar and hunt like a lion? Using this same analogy, another lion would most certainly expect to roar and hunt like any other lion, as it is his nature. You likewise should expect to use your faith to speak to your circumstances and literally create your world just like God did because it is your nature. HE CREATED US JUST LIKE HIM (Genesis 1:26)! In Genesis 1:1-26, God created the heavens and the Earth and everything in it, including man. What I would like to point out is that with everything He created, He actually spoke it into being. Like God, we have the same ability to speak in faith and have those things which we say obey us or come to fruition. In Mark 11:22-24 it states, "And Jesus answering SAITH unto them, Have faith in God. For verily I say unto you, That whosoever shall SAY unto this mountain, Be thou removed, and be thou cast into the sea; and shall not doubt in his heart, but shall believe that those things which he SAITH shall come to pass; he shall (not possibly) have whatsoever he SAITH." Are you following me? Now, watch this! It was not in the saying alone that Jesus said that these things would obey you. He stressed that if you speak and do not DOUBT in your heart, these things shall obey you. Needless to say, God has no doubt in His heart. When He spoke it, this world had to obey. I am sharing with you right now that if you speak with 100% conviction, it will obey you, too! Why will it work for you? Because everything reproduces after its own kind, and God reproduced himself in you. You are like God is. If you do not exercise the power and authority that He has given you, then that is your fault, not His. It would be like a fully grown male lion with a huge beautiful mane being afraid to declare who he is and, as a result, living among the kitty cats. What a pity.

Without faith, it is impossible to please God. Without faith, we cannot even know that He exists because we have never seen Him. We pray totally in faith, acting on the total belief that He is there and can and will provide those things that we 100% believe that we already have. The mind-blowing thing is that it is your faith that actually makes it happen. His word has given us access. The mere fact that we even have peace of mind is faith. We are acting in a manner that suggests that we 100% believe that He will intervene and handle our circumstances.

Because of this peace of mind action (like sleeping in the midst of a storm), He does handle it. Your faith activates the hand of God. WOW! If nothing happens for you, it is because you did nothing. If you do not depress the gas pedal in your car, although the car is fully functional, it will not move.

Okay, now let's go beneath the iceberg, and UNCOVER why it happens as it does. Your subconscious plays a vital role in the process of faith. It is there that God has given us the supreme power, and only requests from this source are transmuted to God as faith petitions. Only to these requests does God respond and return to you the physical manifestation of your desired petition. This is the only language that God responds to. The subconscious mind is the only transmitter of absolute true expression to Him.

Now, this may come as a bit of a shock to some, so let's drill down a bit more as it pertains to this process. Then we will look at a couple of examples.

Here is how it works. You have a thought or desire, which, of course, comes in the form of a thought. This thought will be filtered through your conscious mind, or dominant part of you. In doing so, it will make a determination if you truly agree with this thought or not. It will determine if it is in line with your established belief system. If it is not, then it will be rationalized away. If through this filtration process you or your conscious mind determines that it is in alignment with your belief system, then this thought will be stored in your subconscious as a truth. It will also trigger a signal to your brain, which you possess, to instruct your body to go to work to make it a reality. This is when you will generally feel a sense of joy as though you already have it. Your subconscious mind in conjunction with this emotion will emit vibrations, or faith signals, from you out to God. This is truly what FAITH is. When God receives these vibrations, or faith signals, He will return back to you the exact duplicate of that which He has received. Now watch this! This is why He states, "According to your faith be it on to you." You are the one who initiated the transaction. He returned to you what you emitted to Him. This is also why it is important to be specific when you pray or focus strong thoughts on something. Please note that this is also why God stated that what you bind on

Earth will be bound in heaven, and what you loose on Earth will be loosed in Heaven. Notice that He did not say it in the reverse. Nor did He say it might be.

Let me give you a familiar analogy. There was a time in the United States where gold was being discovered on the West coast. People were migrating from all over to head out west and stake their claim on prosperity. They would get their equipment and begin prospecting. Typically, they would dip a pan with a filtered bottom in the water. This filtered bottom would allow only the gold to stay in and the other non-valuable or inauthentic minerals to pass through. When they actually would see some gold left in their pan they would scream, "Eureka!" They were so excited and filled with joy. Then they would gather their gold and go into town to redeem it for its equivalent cash value. They would get paid precisely what the gold was worth. Not some of the time. All of the time.

This is how the process also works in you. In this analogy, your conscious mind is the pan that filters out things that are of value or in alignment with your established beliefs. What fell through would be the thoughts that you had that you really did not accept as true or were not in alignment with your belief system. What is left after the filtration process is kept or stored. This would be the work of your subconscious mind. This stored material is accepted as a desire and creates some emotion. Your subconscious mind then takes this material to a place where it can be redeemed for its equivalent. This process is known to you and I as FAITH. The person who redeems this material based on the process and gives us precisely the equivalent is our loving God. He doesn't do this sometimes. He does it all the time! Are you with me?

Let's drill down just a bit more. What if you really have a desire for something, however, you just can't seem to make it real to yourself? You want it, but consciously you are not accepting it as a reality, and consequently it doesn't make it to your subconscious and up to God as a faith signal. Well, there is hope. That's right: I said hope. We understand that hope alone will not get it done. However, it is a starting place. Take the thought or desire that you want to receive, and focus on it. If you do this daily and intently, you can cause these thoughts or desires to penetrate your subconscious and, as a result, your petitioned request will reach God, and He will reciprocate by returning to you the physical manifestation of what you sent to Him. This is why God told Joshua to meditate therein day and night. Then you will make yourself prosperous, and then you will have much success. It is through this process that your subconscious will be penetrated, and then you will have the success. This is also why God said "To call those things that be not as though they were. The poor to say they are rich and the weak to say they are strong." God created us and knows that this process will eventually cause those positive thoughts to penetrate your subconscious and, as a result, allow Him to reciprocate back to us. As mentioned earlier it didn't take God 25 years to bring Isaac forth. It took Abraham 25 years to believe that at his age that he and Sarah could conceive a child. It took him 25 years to accept this notion and have it penetrate his subconscious. God is bound by His own word. He said according to YOUR faith be it on to you, not according to HIS faith. As much as God wanted to bring forth many descendants to Abraham, He could not do it until Abraham was able to first accept this promise, have it penetrate his subconscious, and then emit a faith signal or vibration to God which God returned in the form of Isaac. Remember, God had to help him accept this by first changing his name, then showing him the stars in the sky and the grains of sand on the beach. So it is plain to see why the Bible states that faith comes by hearing and hearing and hearing the word of God. It has to penetrate your subconscious, which is the home of your faith.

- *Digest this: (Only thoughts that penetrate your subconscious mind will emit a vibration [faith signal] out to God. This is evidence of what you truly believe that you already have. These things will be reciprocated by God, and the physical manifestation will be returned to you.)*

Strong or Weak Faith...That is the Question

Now let's examine how we make our faith grow. Please keep in mind what happens spiritually and scientifically in the previous chapter, Faith's House...The Subconscious Mind. Here my objective is to get you to truly digest the basic concept so that you may regularly apply and increase your faith. First of all, we know that God said in scripture (Romans 12:3) that He has given everyone the measure of faith. This is 100% accurate. The key here is what we do with the measure we have been given.

There is evidence that we can have strong faith or weak faith, which implies that we have a choice in the matter. The Bible states that Abraham was strong in faith and did not stagger at the promises of God. Now, if you are a male reading this book, then you and I have been given the exact same muscles. I do not have one muscle more than you do, and you don't have one muscle more than I do. It is what we do with the muscles that we have that makes the difference. If I choose to have a sedentary lifestyle, do not eat the proper nutrients, or have an exercise regimen, then I am doing very little to increase my muscle's size and strength. By the same token, if I do eat properly, ensure that I have the proper nutrients, and exercise my body regularly, then the muscles that I have will grow and strengthen. It is the same with faith. We all have the same measure of faith. However, if we eat properly and exercise our faith, it likewise will grow. Now, what is the nourishment for our faith? Of course, it is the word of God, the true breakfast of champions. One of the things that really fortifies this is time to focus, visualize, or meditate daily. I would even go far as to say it is imperative to having strong faith. This is precisely why dream boards work.

Now, in contrast to having strong faith, the Bible clearly illustrates that we can also have weak or little faith. We all know the story about Jesus in the boat with the disciples when they were confronted with a mighty storm (Matthew 8:23-27). Here we clearly see Jesus, being full of faith, a bit frustrated with His disciples. Jesus states, "Oh ye of little faith, how long will I suffer you?" The fact that Jesus states that His disciples have little faith once again implies that they could also have had strong or much faith. Having strong faith or weak faith is up to us.

Looking at the synonymous nature between the way the human body works and how faith works, let me really break down the process of faith. What really happens in the spirit world? How is it that you get faith to grow? You see, getting faith to grow, which will enable it to bring to you precisely what you are believing for, is just like getting your muscles to grow.

You walk into a gym and begin to lift a weight that is comfortable for you. Your objective is to increase your strength. You push the weight as hard as you can for as many repetitions as you can. While doing this, you will exhaust the muscle. In essence, the muscle is actually damaged. It breaks down and becomes sore. During this time, it is a good idea to allow the muscle to rest and ensure that you are replenishing yourself with the proper nutrients so that you can recover and the muscle repairs properly. During this period, the muscle not only repairs itself but also becomes larger in the process. It becomes larger because you have made a demand on it to do more than it was ever required to do before. It is strengthened in anticipation of the continued load or weight that it may be facing in the future. It is now capable of doing much more than it could have prior to going through this process. With consistent weight being added, the body *will repeat this process over and over again, allowing you to become bigger and stronger and capable of handling much more weight. Increased faith grows synonymously. You use your faith to bring into your life something that is easy, for example, believing God for $100. You pray in faith, believing with 100% conviction that you already have it. A message is sent to the brain instructing it to have the body begin to apply the corresponding action to bring it to fruition. As mentioned earlier, emotion will work in conjunction with your subconscious mind, emitting a vibration or faith signal to God. God will in turn emit back to you the physical manifestation of that which you emitted or sent to him. However, please understand that it does not fall out of the sky. You have to uncover it. This uncovering should not create stress because you know, regardless of what you may see, that you already have it. Remember, faith without works is dead. This is especially true when it pertains to healing. So, based on the aforementioned statements, soon enough this $100 is in your pocket. The reason it is downloaded to your subconscious so easily is because it is line with your belief system. You have evidence to support the notion because you have earned $100 before. You got it? Easy,* *right? Now you wish to believe God for $1,000. Now it is time to apply a bit of pressure. So you pray once again according to Mark 11:24. So you believe that you have actually received this $1,000 when you pray. Typically here you will feel a sense of joy. If you do not sense this joy and are actually acting in hope, it will be necessary to meditate day and night on what it is you are desiring. You must do your best in acting as if you already have it. Go shopping and spend freely. This repetition and focus will turn into a true feeling of receiving and once this occurs your subconscious will receive it as though it is already in your possession. As a result, the process of emitting the faith signal to God takes place, and the physical manifestation is reciprocated back to you. Here is where it gets interesting. The time between your faith prayer and the actual physical manifestation of the money is called your patience period. Once again, this is synonymous with your muscles being sore after exertion. Now follow me here. It is during this patience period where most people give up and justify this quitting by saying it must not have been God's will. Please stop blaming God for your lack of steadfastness and your willingness to succumb to mental fatigue. Your mind will always attempt to rationalize* *away the promises of God. This is especially true when you have received a promise or instruction from God to do something GREAT, something that will enable you to make a profound difference in your life and the lives of others. Remember that your conscious mind is looking for evidence within you to support the fact that this can be done. When it finds none, it will rationalize that it is impossible. Your adversary, the devil, will be working overtime to validate your thinking and provide visible evidence to support his case. I say this because this is generally where the battle will take place. In your mind. While you are believing God, your mind is saying, "Everything is not about money." If God wanted you to have the $1,000, you would have already received it. Then the devil puts in his two cents worth: "Anyways, you know that the love of money is the root of all evil. If God blesses you with that money, you will stop coming to Bible study." C'mon, somebody! The truth is, because you didn't receive the money that you prayed for in the timetable that you thought was sufficient, you chose to believe that it was not for you. You gave in to mental fatigue. The devil spoke to your head so hard and so long that you finally agreed with him. Please follow me here. This is not meant to offend or* *judge anyone. However, all scripture is true, 100%. When God states that whatsoever things that we desire, when we pray and believe that we have received those things and we shall have them, it cannot not fail. What things, Wrenwyck? Those things that we 100% believed that we received when we prayed.*

Now, just as it is when increasing your physical strength, what is necessary when increasing your faith is repetition. It is the continual focus and experiencing of having those things manifested in your mind and in turn in our actual reality. The more evidence that you have of its possibility, the easier it is for you to accept it into your subconscious and emit a faith signal that will result into its physical manifestation 100% of the time. The truth is, you will need to spend more time imagining and less time working. When I state to experience things in actual reality, I mean to go and test drive the car. It has to become real to you. Go walk around in that house. Take a picture of it and focus on it so intently that you open doors in your house expecting to see the rooms in the house that you desire. This builds your faith and this also expedites the process of having things downloaded to your subconscious and emitted up to God.

The daily practice of focusing on what you desire or thinking on purpose will enable you to more vividly and keenly visualize such requests and, as a result, more expeditiously have them manifested in your life. Each successful manifestation will result in stronger faith. Are you following me? Remember, David's faith was strengthened by defeating a lion and a bear prior to killing Goliath. Abraham's faith was strengthened by his name being changed and getting a vivid image of his descendants in the stars of the sky and the grains of sands on the beach.

God's word will not return to Him void. He said, whatsoever you desire, believe when you pray that you have already received it. That is it. This is scripture and law, and is truthfully not a matter of God's will. God always says yes, we say no. Okay, now you are feeling funny. You are feeling weird because I have taken away a sacred cow. You see, prior to reading this book you could always blame your lack of receiving on God. You could always fall back on, "It wasn't His will." The truth is, it has nothing to do with His will at all. It has to do with your faith or lack thereof, the same way that your muscles have no choice but to grow if you continue to exercise them and give them the proper amount of protein and nutrients. So, it is with your faith. God says "But be joyful and confident in this Great Affirmation, that ALL the Promises of God in Him are Yea, and in Him Amen, unto the Glory of God by us" (2 Corinthians 1:20). All answers are yea and amen. I know that you have heard people say that your faith is not based on a feeling. This is true, but I believe that your praying in releasing this faith is. You must pray with a bit of emotion, some enthusiasm, if you will. Enthusiasm was originally defined as <u>inspiration</u> or <u>possession</u> by the <u>presence of God</u>. You must be able to get into the spirit in order to penetrate the ears and heart of God. Once again, emitting with emotion from the subconscious, OTHERWISE YOU ARE MERELY TALKING. Many bodybuilders take supplements like nitric oxide to allow their bodies to be able to complete more repetitions and increase the growth process. Your supplements are the emotion you experience when you truly pray in faith. I am not suggesting that you are jumping up and down or completing perfect somersaults, but I mean a sense of joy that you recognize within yourself, the kind that makes you smile for seemingly no reason and walk a bit more upright. I must say that I question whether or not you truly believe that you have received from God and do not feel a sense of joy. Are you with me? C'mon now. You mean to tell me that if you need $10,000 because you are heading for foreclosure, your wife is upset and your children not speaking to you? You cannot sleep, and barely eat. Then you get a call from your Aunt Gladys, and she says to you, "Hey, don't give it a second thought. I have the money, and I will pay it tomorrow." You don't think there would be some expression of joy? You would be smiling and probably shouting, "Halleluiah!" Why? Because you believe that you have already received it, even though at the time of the call you had seen no money. If you can get excited about Aunt Gladys' promise, why not about God's? Are you following me?

When we really drill down to the core, what we are really stating when we talk about faith is trust. Trusting God that He will do what He said in His word. Trusting that, when you prayed and believed that it was already done, you had the confidence to act without seeing any visual evidence that it has come to fruition. The only evidence that you have is your faith. Uh oh...that means it is back to you. Let me share a brief story with you that epitomizes what I am stating. This will be very pertinent to those who are believing God for a house. In 1994,

I found myself unemployed after being in management with a very prominent company for many years. Quite naturally, I wasn't feeling particularly joyful, as month after month passed by without finding suitable employment. I must admit that, although I was certainly believing in God, that this situation was already rectified, I felt like crap each time my wife went out of that door to work, and I was left there looking crazy and watching the daytime soap operas. This was certainly what I refer to as my Daniel period. Yes, I was in the lion's den. If you have ever found yourself in the lion's den whether it was unemployment or something else, then you know it is no joke. On top of that, I had applied for unemployment, and it was denied. Can I get real with you for a moment? Now I was mad. I really wanted to hurt somebody. Anyways, it was at this time the Holy Spirit reminded me once again of God's word. He stated, as only He can, to never accept any situation without considering the God factor. He reminded me that God said that whatsoever things that you desire, when you pray believe that you have received it, and ye shall have it. No stipulations. It didn't matter if you were tall, short, black, white, popeyed, or bowlegged. No offense, mind you. The only stipulation was that you were

100% convinced that you already had it when you prayed. I went out to my bathroom, and I prayed. I didn't just want that unemployment money: I had to have it. I went back the next week, and I was denied again. Finally, they decided to give me a hearing, and, once again, I was denied. To be honest, all of this negativity did nothing but make me more determined. To make a long story short, for seven months I was denied, and then suddenly (isn't it amazing how God always does things suddenly?) I received a letter from the state of North Carolina that stated that I was approved. Not only would I receive compensation, but they would also make it retroactive back to the date of my initial application. Tell me that God's word is not real. I got a lump sum check for the entire seven months. Now, watch this. When I prayed for the money, I truly believed that I had already received it. It was this belief that enabled me to continue to pursue it. I do not want to get in to it too much in this book, but at times there is spiritual opposition to your prayers. Keep pursuing your request until it has manifested. If you prayed in faith, it has already been answered and is on its way. The only thing your adversary can do is attempt to slow it down. He does this in hopes of stealing your faith. He is resting on the fact that if you do not receive it in a timely manner, then your faith gives way to fear. They can never occupy the same place at the same time. One must go. The determining factor of which remains or vacates is totally up to you. This is why, at times, it seems like things appear to happen suddenly. It's like an electrical malfunction in your home. The power has not been turned off at the electric company; it is still flowing. Unfortunately, there is a wire cut within the physical structure of your house. This mishap is opposing or preventing the electricity from flowing to your home as it should. Once this mishap is corrected, suddenly your power is restored. You got it. Here is the key: NEVER, NEVER, NEVER give up. Your faith will see you through. Remember, if you believe that you already have it, then how can you quit? You see, the devil is hoping that you do not believe that it will show up. It has no choice.

Back to how to get your home. Now that I had received the unemployment compensation, I was fired up but still unemployed. It was at this time that God shared with me that I should purchase a bigger house. He stated that it should be three times the size of the one I currently owned. As you might imagine, my mind got involved right away, and I rationalized away this thought. My mind said, "You know, Wrenwyck, they do not loan money for homes to people who do not have jobs." As soon as I heard those words, I immediately agreed with them and was accepting of the thought. However, that small voice reminded me once again that God did not place any stipulations on the words of Mark 11:24, except one: "Believe when you pray." The whatsoever in the scripture means that there is nothing too rare, too expensive, or out of His reach. How can anything be out of the reach of God? Please keep in mind that your part is to accept it as truth and act on your faith. God will do whatever is necessary to perform His word. With His word rooted deep within my spirit (subconscious), I couldn't wait until Wanda, my wife of 11 years at that time, came home. Man, I was so excited! I had already prepared some Hamburger Helper, broccoli with cheese, and corn on the cob, and Hungry Jack biscuits were in the oven. Remember, this was 1994. I was so proud of myself I didn't know what to do. So then I led her in to the den, and I said, "Guess what God told me today?" She looked at me and said, "That you will be getting a job." I didn't even flinch. I said, "No, but He did say that we should purchase another house, and it should be three times the size of this one."

I am going by memory here, but I believe that she started crying. She didn't want any biscuits, Hamburger Helper, or anything. She looked at me and said, "Rick, I know you are a man of faith, but they do not give houses to people who do not have jobs." Ummmmmm, it seemed like I had heard those words before. Now, as the head, you must exercise wisdom in communicating with your wife. Please know that financial security is number one on her list of needs. At the moment, at least in this scenario, I was not working, which in turn created some undue stress on her. I simply said, "I understand how this must sound to you. I must admit that when I first heard it, I felt the same way. Come on over here and let's partake of this Hamburger Helper and biscuits, and we can discuss it later." Then, you need to start praying for God to grant you more wisdom in communicating with your wife and for her to hear His voice as well. One thing I will strongly recommend here is, as married couples, you want to come into agreement with each other. Remember, one can put 1,000 to flight, but two can put 10,000 to flight. You are much stronger together than you are apart. Now, let me speed this story up a bit. Once Wanda and I were able to come into agreement and prayed in faith, believing that we had already received exactly what it was that God had shared with me, we were on our way. It is very important to be specific here. You will, 100% of the time, not get necessarily what you want but rather what you 100% believe that you already have. When we prayed, we requested specifics about the size and look of the house. Are you still following me? I need to share with you this: When you begin to believe in God for big things, expect some opposition. This opposition comes in many forms. At times it may be a well meaning family member or friend. Do you think that the adversary, the devil, is just going to allow you to receive things from God and give him open glory without a fight? Probably not. You see, by you receiving things from God and openly giving Him praise and glory, testifying of His goodness, this just might build up faith in other people and, before you know it, believers will start prospering and paying churches off. You know, the devil is not going to simply sit there and allow this to happen. His entire arsenal will be pointed at one place, your head, but, more specifically, your mind. He and his cohorts are going to tell you so many things about yourself, your finances, your culture, your credit, and, in my case, lack of employment. To make it worse, they have tangible evidence to show you just in case you thought they were making it up. We had every obstacle known to man come against us. However, we were reminded by the Holy Spirit that greater is He that is in us than He that is in this world. We knew by His word that what we truly believed we had already received, and there was not an entity in the world that could stop it. To bring closure to this story, after much opposition we were successful in purchasing the home that we had specifically asked for, I mean down to the precise square footage. Not one square foot more or less. God created the physical manifestation of precisely what we had emitted to Him through vibrations from our subconscious minds, also known as our faith. Isn't this awesome?!

- *Digest this: (Having strong or weak faith is not a choice made by God, but a decision made by you.)*

Keep Your Healing...Turn off the TV

"What I have feared most has come upon me." Job 3:25

Hey, I'm just going to give it to you straight. YOU DO NOT HAVE TO BE SICK! Unfortunately, a great deal of sickness is self-induced. Please know that it is not my intent to be insensitive here. What I state here I state out of love and an unwavering desire to see you free from a bondage that has long been removed. Why do we remain enslaved by mental shackles that oppress and preclude us from glorifying God with our bodies? I'll tell you why. The reason is that we either are not aware or do not believe that we have been emancipated. I have had family members that are ill and have had good friends who have died from illness. This is precisely why I am so adamant, if not radical, about the matter. I am infringed at the notion that we have been led to believe that being sick is just a part of life. NOT TRUE! NOT TRUE! NOT TRUE! The issue here, as with everything else, is that, for many of us, we have accepted it as being true. As you know, if you believe that it is so, then it is so. The power is in you. Many of *us purchase medications when there is an advertised sale in the anticipation and expectation of being ill at some point in the future. Guess what? You are right! You have acted on your faith and, sure enough, it has come to pass. When the sickness shows up, you commend yourself by stating, "Man, it sure was a good thing that I purchased that medication when I did." I'll give you a minute here. You got it? Exactly. You were actually working in concert with the one who comes to kill, steal, and destroy. Man, I bet he is proud of you. Next week, he will make sure that there are more medications on sale so that you might act on your faith for sickness once more. At this point, it becomes a habit, and sickness is a part of your life. By the way, when that medication goes on sale again, please do not call and share it with anyone. While I am on the subject, it is very important to discontinue the practice of personalizing the illnesses that your doctor may have diagnosed you as having. For example, "my high blood pressure," "my diabetes," or "my arthritis." It does not belong to you. It has been delivered to the wrong house. Are you following me? If you do not accept this notion of everyone must get sick as a truth, then it is not true for the same reason. The power is in you and, according to YOUR faith, be it on to* you. I do not recall a single scripture where it mentions Jesus being ill. He is our example, is He not? I accept with everything that is in me that by Jesus' stripes we were healed. Quite naturally, that would mean that we are healed now. I just do not know any other way to interpret that scripture. Either we accept it as true, or we do not. The problem with most people is that they receive tangible evidence that suggests the contrary and accept this as being true. In other words, they have more faith in the x-ray that they receive than they do in God's word. To exacerbate the situation, they add fear to it by fearing the prognosis based on the x-ray they saw. This is what the devil calls his "Manhattan Project," "Atomic Bomb," "Weapon of Mass Destruction," or "Double Whammy." It leaves individuals in shock and awe. They are left with a feeling of hopelessness and despair. The ironic thing about many of these situations is that many felt absolutely fine prior to receiving the news.

Let me give you an example. Let's say that I tell you that I have paid your mortgage completely off, and now you no longer owe anything to the lending institution. As a matter of fact, I send you the property deed. You are elated! You are elated until four months later when the bank sends you an invoice and states that you are behind on your mortgage and owe for the full four months. If they do not receive it in 45 days, they will begin foreclosure procedures. Uh oh! "Man, I don't believe this. I thought Wrenwyck said that he paid it in full. I am so upset. How could he say that, and then I get this notice? As I look closer at this property deed, it doesn't even look valid. It's not signed by the President or anything. To make matters worse, I already purchased a new car and some Prada shoes. It's over now! I'm going to be in the streets. I wonder if Mommy and Daddy will let me move back home?" This is how we react to the news of illness even though Jesus has told us that by His stripes we were healed. Because man has given us tangible evidence we fear and do not stand on Jesus' word. What should happen in the aforementioned scenario is that we should look at the notice from the bank, smile, and say, "Please! I know this is an error. As a matter of fact, Wrenwyck sent me the property deed. I'm going to get in my new car, put on my Prada shoes, and go down to the bank and straighten this out. This is unacceptable, and I will never send them another mortgage payment. My house is paid in FULL!"

Please get this. In the same way that we activate the power of faith in our lives by believing that we have already received what we prayed for, the same is true when we activate fear. It will work in precisely the same way to bring you what you DO NOT want. Remember, what you think about you bring about.

Lets apply our formula for faith to healing. Okay, so you get a word that states by His stripes you are healed. You believe this, and it is in alignment with your established belief system. Your conscious mind accepts it, and it is downloaded to your subconscious. Your subconscious will emit with emotion a vibration (faith signal) out to God that you are 100% healed. God will receive this emitted vibration and reciprocate the exact equivalent back to you: the physical manifestation of what you emitted to him. In this case, it is a body that is 100% healed. Please note that the exact process takes place when you emit a signal that states that you are not healed based on the doctor's report and visible x-rays. A faith signal is once again emitted up to God but this time in the form of fear. Fear is faith for what you do not want. As before, God will reciprocate back to you what you had faith for. In this case, it is sickness. Remember, in many cases when Jesus was confronted with individuals being ill, He would first state to them to "Fear not." He understood the power of their fears. This is also why He would ask at times for people to leave the room when healing. He knew that if they had unbelief, then their subconscious would be collectively emitting signals up to God that were contrary to His own. They, in fact, would be working against Him. Are you following me?

Once again, all too often individuals are feeling great, then once they receive this evil report and accept it as a truth, they are gone in six months. Whatever you allow to penetrate your subconscious as truth, your subconscious will accept it and cooperate with it. Soon your body will begin to exhibit the symptoms associated with whatever it is that you have accepted.

I am aware that at times we are attacked. So I am not suggesting that the mailman will not show up to your door from time to time with a package that is not for you, because he will. What I am saying is, kindly let him know that he is at the wrong house, and you cannot accept it. Whatever you do, DO NOT SIGN FOR IT. Once you do, it is yours. Please know it is how you respond to the mailman that makes all the difference. You will either have faith in Jesus' word or exhibit fear based on the prognosis. You cannot do both. Faith and fear cannot exist in the same place at the same time. The one that stays is totally up to you. Job stated, "For the thing which I greatly feared is come upon me, and that which I was afraid of is come unto me." He is 100% correct. This scripture is so important, as it pertains to maintaining your health. Also please keep in mind that this was before Jesus went to the cross and stated that by His stripes we were healed. We would probably agree that most of the time when individuals get a negative or evil report, it produces fear. It is important to recognize this and not give in to it. I have personally had to stand on the word of God more than one time for my healing. In 2001, I was a vice president at a global internet marketing company. I was really enjoying my tenure there, and the company was experiencing much success. During this period, in addition to my corporate responsibilities, one of the things that I would do was to go out in the field to teach, motivate, and inspire our distributors. On this occasion I was going to Minnesota (Go Vikings!) to speak at a regional event. Approximately three weeks prior, I began to have *great abdominal pains and excessive trips to the bathroom. Are you following me? The pain was so severe that it actually hurt to drink water. Quite naturally, I was losing quite a large amount of weight and looked very sickly because I was so dehydrated. I must say that I am not one to go the doctor's office very often, but while I was in Minnesota, the pain was so severe that I called my wife and asked her to make an appointment for me. Praise God that I was able to speak at the regional convention, and it was very successful. Upon returning home, I did visit the doctor, and they told me I was healthy as a horse, and I am quoting him. I in turn replied, "That may be so. However, I am in extreme pain and have lost about 20 pounds in three weeks." He asked me to take a stool sample and return in a week. I did so only to be told they could find nothing. Okay, this is about the time that the devil begins to speak to your mind. He was telling me all sorts of things. "You know it is probably some sort of stomach cancer. So and so had the same thing. As a matter of fact, they weren't in nearly as much pain as you are in and didn't lose any weight." Then he got into more detail. "Did you see the way the doctor looked at you? He looked sad, as if he didn't want to say what was really wrong.*

He's probably waiting for more tests before he shares that it has spread." That was it. I had enough. It was time to roll up my sleeves and fight! I have too much joy and have way too much to do for this mess. This package does not belong to me and I command it in the name of Jesus to GO! Then I got radical. It is written that "Man shall not live by bread alone but by every word that proceedeth out of the mouth of God." Jesus said by His stripes, "I am healed and he cannot not lie." I am standing on His word, and this, too, must pass! The thing is, I meant every word of it and knew with 100% certainty that I was healed. I returned to the doctor's office and this time was seen by someone new. He could tell I was fired up. He asked me if I had taken any antibiotics in the past 90 days. I thought for a moment and remembered a root canal that I had in which antibiotics were given to me. He left the room for about 20 minutes, which of course felt like one hour. He walked in, looked at me and said, "Keep believing God for your healing." Now, c'mon! You know doctors do not say that. He handed me a prescription and left. The prescription was for more antibiotics. Needless to say, I never saw that doctor again, and the pain and all symptoms were gone in a matter of days. I'm telling you that it is

ACCORDING TO YOUR FAITH! Jesus already did the work on the cross. I give God the glory that I have never been sick since that time. To date in my 52 years, I have only been to the hospital once, and that was because I broke my ankle playing high school basketball. I believe His word with everything that is in me and speak it over my life every day. I am so grateful, and it is this consistent attitude of gratefulness and worship which gives me better health each day. The more that I am grateful, the more that I have to be grateful for. I lift weights and run every day. Each day, as I complete my run, I raise my hands to heaven and give thanks for the fact that I am strong and can run. I share with God each day that I want to glorify Him in my spirit and in my body. I graduated from Westover Senior High School in Fayetteville, NC in 1978. I weighed 165 pounds at six feet tall. Today, 34 years later, and after two decades of marriage, two gorgeous daughters, and a very successful corporate career, I'm still six feet and weigh 165 pounds. All we have to do is maintain our bodies and stand on His word that we are healed. He did the hard part by sacrificing on the cross to give it to me. Are you getting this? I can just hear Jesus now saying, "You mean to tell me that I endured all of that *suffering in my flesh, absorbing lash after lash so that you can be healed, and you let someone take it from you?" I'll let you answer that one for yourself. The truth is, it is up to you.*

Now, one of the things that I personally do to help me in this matter is this. Whenever I am watching television, which is very rare, and I see a report about some new illness or how to prevent this or that or more studies on cancer, I quickly change the channel or turn the TV off. That's right! I do not need to hear that. What does that information have to do with me, if by Jesus' stripes, I am healed? So now you are thinking, "But it is better to be informed so you can prevent it." How is knowing that others are receiving misdirected packages to their homes going to prevent the mailman from delivering the wrong package to me? As a matter of fact, the more you know about these occurrences, the more you will begin to think about it and eventually expect it to happen to you. I can assure you that you will not be disappointed. Soon enough you will get the wrong package, too, and state, "I knew this would happen" as if you had nothing to do with it. Wake up. You are more powerful than you think. From the abundance of the heart, the mouth will speak, and what you believe in your heart and

*speak with your mouth shall be so. I am sharing with you that the saturation of information concerning illness causes many people to fear, and that fear actually brings the illness to them. Once again, remember what Job said: "What I feared most has come upon me." Hey, what you think about you bring about. One more thing. Faith cometh by hearing, and so does fear. Now, if more information on illness is better for us, with the internet and television saturating our minds with it, wouldn't that mean that we should have less illness? Watch this. The WHO (World Health Organization) was asked this question and here is their response.
(1 April 2008)*

Q: Are the number of cancer cases increasing or decreasing in the world?

A: Cancer is a leading cause of death worldwide, and the total number of cases globally is increasing.

The number of global cancer deaths is projected to increase 45% from 2007 to 2030 (from 7.9 million to 11.5 million deaths). It is influenced in part by an increasing and aging global population. The estimated rise takes into account expected slight declines in death rates for some cancers in high-resource countries. New cases of cancer in the same period are estimated to jump from 11.3 million in 2007 to 15.5 million in 2030.

Please do not misunderstand. Certainly, some of the information has its place and is beneficial. However, the saturation of it to some individuals creates fear, and that fear perpetuates more fear. Fear acts just like faith. It will draw to you what you are fearful of. Guard your eyes and your ears. In this way, you will also guard your mind. Do not ever accept illness. It is not for you. If it happens to show up on your door, do not keep it.

One of the best examples of this is the woman with the issue of blood. The story speaks about a woman who had been suffering with an issue of blood for 12 years. It goes on to state that she spent all that she had on doctors and still had the same illness. Now, in those days, a woman who had blood issues, most likely menstruation, was said to be unclean. Can you imagine being unclean for 12 years? Due to her condition, she did not dare approach Jesus and openly ask for healing. Instead, she fought her way through the crowd in an attempt to merely touch His clothing. She believed with 100% certainty that if she could merely touch His clothing, she would be healed. Now, she did not just stand still and believe. She acted on her belief by fighting her way through the crowd and actually touching His clothing. This is true faith. The evidence of your belief is the action that you take. Now watch this. Jesus never saw her before she touched Him. He only acknowledged her after her confession. So here we can plainly see that Jesus had no premeditation in healing her, and actually He had nothing to do with it, except of course being the possessor of the healing power. He didn't even know she was there. As Jesus stated himself, it was her faith that healed her. Her faith being emitted from her subconscious as a vibration went from her to Jesus, being God. As discussed in our process, once Jesus received this vibration or faith signal, He reciprocated back to her. He even said Himself, who touched me, not because He felt her hand on His garment. No, it was because He *felt the vibration or virtue come out of Him to heal her. Her faith activated the healing power of Jesus. This provides evidence that we all have access to the healing power of Jesus. The only difference is whether we truly believe that we will be healed. In those days, Jesus healed the people on individual occasions. However, when He went to the cross, He stated that by His stripes we were healed. Who was healed? All who believe on Him and accept this word as being truth. The acceptance is demonstrated by your faith.*

Hey, let's take a bit of a side journey here! There is another message in this story. The Bible states that she had an issue of blood and was obviously unclean. This story is also a metaphor for salvation in that the spiritually unclean also have an issue of blood. They have not accepted Jesus as Lord and Savior, and their sins have not been remised by the shedding of Jesus' blood. You see, in this way they have a blood issue because the shedding of their blood will not remit their sins and, until they accept Jesus, they remain spiritually unclean. Many people today still have a blood issue and remain spiritually unclean. To take it one step further, Jesus asked "Who touched me?" Do you think that He really did not know? Of course He did after He felt the virtue come out of Him. However, in Romans 9:10 it states, and I am paraphrasing, that you must believe in your heart and confess with your mouth that Jesus is your Lord and Savior. I believe that Jesus asked who touched me so the lady who had obviously already believed in her heart could now confess with her mouth.

Some have taught that God will heal some and some He will not. I am stating that this is NOT TRUE! He did not state that by His stripes some are healed. It is God's will that all be healed. He has given us all access to this precious healing power. However, like the woman with the issue of blood, we must believe that we have it and even fight to keep it if necessary.

Let me state for the record that I am not suggesting that we be ignorant as it pertains to our health, nor am I suggesting that we do not visit our physicians. What I am stating is to please be mindful of the amount of time that you spend listening to information and watching programs about sickness and diseases. It can create fear and, as stated earlier, this fear will act just like faith, and it will surely bring to you whatever it is that you are fearful about. Stand boldly on the word of God, and do not be fearful of saying that I am totally healed and will not accept anything less. If the mailman leaves you a package that does not belong to you, do not sign for it and state everyday that, "This too shall pass." You will look out on your porch one morning, and it will be gone.

- *Digest this: (Sickness is not for you. You must guard your heart and mind to ensure that you are not inundated with information that can potentially create fear. Fear acts just like faith, in that it will draw to you precisely what you are fearful of. What you think about, you bring about.)*

Above All, Prosper and Be in Good Health

Those of you who have children can certainly relate to the feeling you get when your child does something that makes you proud. It doesn't matter if it's singing the solo in the Easter play or being the proud tree in the production of Snow White. When your child takes the stage and performs their part in their own unique way, a sense of pride rises up in you that could fill an arena. You are literally beaming with joy at the fact that your little creation, the one that you birthed, nourished, changed, taught, and loved so much, has actually done something of significance in relation to their age. Just the thought that this is only the beginning creates a vision in your mind of what they will become. Even in the event that they may have a mishap and forget a line, you see right past that. The mishap that they concern themselves with fails to distract from the vision you so vividly see. Thinking about this, I am reminded of the times when my own daughters Natasha, now 30, and Naomi, now 24, were dancing in the Harris-Mintz recital in Greensboro, North Carolina.

Man, I was so proud. I had my camera ready as I sat there in great anticipation of my girls taking the stage. Then, after about two or three dances, there she was. Natasha had enough charisma to fill Carnegie Hall. She stepped right up with her little tap shoes on, pointed her finger like a gun, stomped her small foot once, and said, "Bang! Bang!" Hey, I want you to know that there wasn't another little girl on planet Earth that could say "Bang! Bang!" like that. New York better get ready. Later in the program, my youngest daughter, Naomi, came out. She ran to the middle of the stage, jumped about three inches off the floor, and just kept right on running. To me, it was the beginning of an Olympian. Surely she would grace the cover of Sports Illustrated and monopolize the highlights on ESPN. They would do these things of course prior to receiving their doctorate degrees. What I am saying is that although they were quite young, I could see that they were blessed with gifts and talents, and I could actually see them at that time as mature adults fulfilling their potential. Their gifts were an indication of what was to come. It was obvious by the natural way that they did things. These gifts were given by God, and if they choose to operate in them they will be cooperating with

Him and maximizing the gifts with which He has endowed them. God sees all of us in the same manner that I saw my daughters, although they were still children. You see, God is not limited by time and sees us all as we shall be, grown into maturity and cooperating with Him as it relates to maximizing our gifts. You see, in that place and time is where we are truly blessed and truly bless others. Giving of your gift is the truest expression of Love. In addition, when we operate in these gifts and acknowledge God for them, He is glorified. I have found that what you use to glorify God will also prosper you. You, too, have been endowed with unique gifts and talents. Isn't it awesome to know that you are Great and possess a calling in your life? If you are not aware of the awesome gifts that you possess, then all you need to do is simply ask God to reveal them to you. A clue will be the things that you seem to do naturally. The things that bring you joy and you are quite passionate about. The truth is that it has already been revealed and just seems too big or too good to be true. I can tell you this with 100% certainty that if it does not seem too good to be true, then it is probably not it. If it is not big enough that you will need His help to bring it to fruition, then I would say to keep searching. What God has imparted in you is great! I am certain that you have felt this deep down inside of you. You have heard the voices from time to time tell you certain things, and when you heard it, it felt so good. It came as a thought, but, as opposed to meditating and focusing on it, you found a way to rationalize it away. It sounded just too good. It felt too much like a dream. If you had only realized that all you had to do was say, "Yes," and that's it! All you have to do is make a decision to do it. Simply say "Yes, God, I believe I will." You see, God always says yes. You say no. Not only does He say yes, He also designs a universal plan to ensure that you are successful in your endeavor. Let me use this analogy to demonstrate what I mean. Let's say that it is shared with you that you should take a trip from Fayetteville, North Carolina to Los Angeles, California. You feel like, "Man, that would be awesome" and actually say, "Yes, God, I believe I will." You begin to think about the trip all the time. You have the stamina and transportation. However, you have no idea how to get there. No worries; God acts as your GPS. Just take a leap of faith in the direction of your destination. Go West! Like your car's GPS, the first thing God does is identify where you are. Then He immediately creates the best route for you to get there. Now, please note that I did not say the quickest route. I said the best route. As you are traveling, you find there are people and places along the way that enlighten and empower you in some sense, and you have experiences that create growth. You may have a radiator go bad or a flat tire or two. Either way, you will find them to be invaluable learning experiences. So simply count them all as joy. Along the way, you will make friends with strangers who are willing to give you food and direction. You will likewise meet people that you are able to bless from the lessons that you have learned. You see, this is why it is necessary to take the best route and not the quickest. There are specific experiences you will have along the way that are necessary for you to be successful in making it to your destination and fulfilling your calling. Had you taken a shortcut, these experiences and blessings could have been missed.

In saying this, you are not unlike many individuals that decide that this way is just too slow. You make a decision that, although God meant well, you might need to step in and assist Him. I mean, it is not as though you are a novice at this point. So even though the GPS says make a right turn in 3.5 miles, you make a decision to make a right in 1 mile. You can cut across the interstate and get ahead by 50 miles. What a great idea! You are feeling fantastic! You are singing along with your favorite CDs, the scenery is beautiful, and you find a diner off the highway that has all-you-can-eat pancakes. Life is AWESOME! It is awesome until... until you realize that the road in which you are traveling has a bridge out on it. The way to get to your destination is to go back in the direction that you came. The only issue is that you are not totally certain how to get back. No worries! All that is necessary is to resort back to the GPS, which, in this case, is God. Simply ask Him for help and direction, and it is freely given. Remember, God never leaves or forsakes us. He is full of Grace and Mercy. Just like your car's GPS, He will re-route you and get you back on the right path. You see, even if you make mistakes, fall asleep, or are just plain disobedient, God loves you and will be with you as long as you are willing to continue along the way. You can only fail if you quit. Regardless of what your calling is, keep focusing, concentrating, and working toward it. You are closer to attaining it than you think. Whatever you do, do not abort the dream that God has impregnated you *with. Although there may be some morning sickness, pain, and discomfort along the way, please know that in its season you will deliver, and your dreams and aspirations will be realized. When you focus on the joy of the birth, the labor seems to be insignificant!*

I would be remiss if I did not share that the lifestyle that you live is totally up to you, not God. In 3 John 1:2, He said, "Above all I want you to prosper and be in good health even as your soul prospers." Now, get this. When He says "even as," what He is saying is prosper and be in good health to the equivalent that your soul or mind part of you prospers. Your soul or mind has to prosper before you will ever realize any prosperity in your life. Poverty and prosperity can always be found in the same place: in your mind. You must be prosperity-minded in order to attain prosperity. It is drawn by and to those who are 100% convinced that they already have it. This is why the rich get richer and the poor get poorer. This is why one man can make one million dollars, lose it all, and create it all again, while another will have difficulty making one hundred thousand dollars. Please understand that it is mental not physical. The key to this life is not working hard but thinking right. This is also why He said to be not conformed but be transformed by the renewing of your mind. You have to come out of the matrix. As you renew your mind to who you are and the power you possess, you will be empowered to simply imagine with great and consistent thought, followed by the corresponding action, and have those things come to you. It is in the genuine belief that you have already received that compels you to act. You can simply ask in faith (believe it is done when you ask) and trust that which you believed you received when you prayed, you will most assuredly have. This is the awesome power that God has created us with. If your petitions or desires do not come to pass, it is not God. It is you. Now, I believe that you should pray God's will, but in the event that you do not receive what you want, do not blame your lack of perseverance and faith on God's will. God's will has nothing to do with you having a Mercedes or a Ford. Show me in the Bible where God has ever wanted anything but abundance for his children. According to YOUR faith be it on to you. That is it!

Look at it like this. See God as this mighty ocean. In this ocean is an unlimited supply of all sorts of marine life. Everything from minnows to mackerel from whitefish to whales. It really doesn't matter which fish you prefer because you have access to all of them. Some will say, "May I have lobster?" and others will ask for calamari. The response will be, "According to your faith be it on to you." The only difference is what you have faith for. You see, if you want minnows, you can fish in shallow water, and it doesn't require much effort, equipment, or expertise. Now if you want a barracuda, then I would suggest that you make sure that you have a boat, certainly powerful equipment, expertise, and experience. However, the question isn't whether or not you can have one. The question is only whether you are willing to do the things that are necessary to catch one. You will not find barracudas in shallow water. Remember what Jesus told Peter after Peter had been fishing all day and caught nothing? He said to cast your nets again, but this time go out into the deep. This is where you will find your harvest.

The same is true as it relates to having luxury cars, million-dollar homes, expensive clothes, or whatever type of things that you desire. The only question is whether you are willing to do the things that are necessary to attain them. It is all up to you. By the way, the same goes for your health.

The bottom line is that God does not care what type of car you drive. He does not care what type of house, boat, clothes, or furniture you own. He simply does not want these things to own you. If you act on what you believe as if you already have it, then it will inevitably be yours. God has already done His part by giving you access to all things. Now activate the awesome God power (faith) in you, and make your most intimate dreams come to fruition. In doing so you will become a blessing to others and glorify God. God gets no glory from you being poor and having lack of resources in your life. This is why He has gone to great lengths in the Bible to stress a life of abundance. Nothing that God has for you is adequate. Everything He has and does is exceedingly and abundantly more than enough. Your cup should continually run over. You cannot be a blessing if you are not blessed.

It has been my objective with this book to touch your life in such a profound way as to compel YOU to pursue YOU, and in doing so to uncover your life's journey. A journey of growth and enlightenment, not focused on solely attaining success, but of revealing significance. It is only in the discovery and fulfillment of this significance, this purpose, that you will find true success. I *pray that you cooperate with God in your gifts and calling. Allow Him to play the role of the GPS, providing direction, clarity, and empowering you with the tools, thoughts, and language necessary to evoke action and create successful thinking, resulting in modified behavior. Collaborate with Him in your innate quest to not solely making a life but in profoundly making a difference. Endeavor to uncover your genius, leaving your unique footprints in the sand and ultimately receiving the satisfaction of knowing that this world is just a bit better because you, too, are here. The world is waiting. The POWER to impact it is in you.*

- *Digest this: (Health and prosperity should not be a choice but rather an expectation.)*

P.S. Please take time to teach these concepts to your children. Let's not allow another generation to pass without imparting this awesome revelation in them of who they truly are and the power that they have been endowed with. Ensure that your children understand that they are in total control of their destinies so that they will be responsible and accountable for the life they live. Create an expectation of greatness in your children so that they will shun the mundane and refuse to accept mediocrity. Teach them to work certainly, but more importantly to dream. It is in the aspiration of the dream that will compel them to work. Make sure that they know that as God is, they are!

Make sure that you, as well as your children, know that when you truly have faith, there is no need for a plan B. Success in your life is guaranteed. I want to expand on this and share the steps necessary to make this happen.....and I will, in Baby Food (digestible concepts) Book 2.

With Much Love,
Wrenwyck

Wrenwyck Williams

Wrenwyck Williams, is first and foremost a Man of God and minister of the gospel of Jesus Christ. He is a firm believer that God has created us all for greatness and it is just a matter of enlightening, creating awareness of who we truly are, and of the power that has been innately created inside of us. He believes that we were created in God's image and likeness and as God is, so we are.

He is an extremely effective life strategist who specializes in Spiritual, Executive, Personal, and Health and Wellness coaching.

Wrenwyck has been a highly sought after and successful corporate executive for the past 27 years, both domestically and internationally. He has worked his way up from entry level associate to President/CEO during his tenure with multi-million dollar corporations. Along the way he has earned many accolades and awards for his exceptional leadership and ability meet and exceed established goals. He has also been in ministry in various capacities for the past 23 years. This knowledge and experience has given him the insight necessary to understand the mindset and plight of the executive as well as parishioners and empowered him to be able to create strategies that will enable them both to meet their professional and personal and spiritual goals.

In addition Wrenwyck is a licensed NLP practitioner and utilizes these techniques to provide clients with a greater capacity to produce results and a greater confidence in their ability to do so. Whether it is weight loss, unwanted habits, poor relationships or low self-esteem, he has experienced excellent results from clients with whom he has provided service for.

He is also a highly recognized and award winning international public speaker (Toastmasters International-DTM) and trainer. His inspirational messages and charismatic style has impacted the lives of thousands.

"Understanding my unquenchable passion and desire to see individuals fulfill their potential is easy,....... I simply love God and love all people."

Wrenwyck Williams

"The evidence of your belief is the action that you take."

Wrenwyck Williams

Please visit my site at www.babyfoodbook.net and register for a free gift and Trial Membership.

Be Blessed,

Wrenwyck Williams

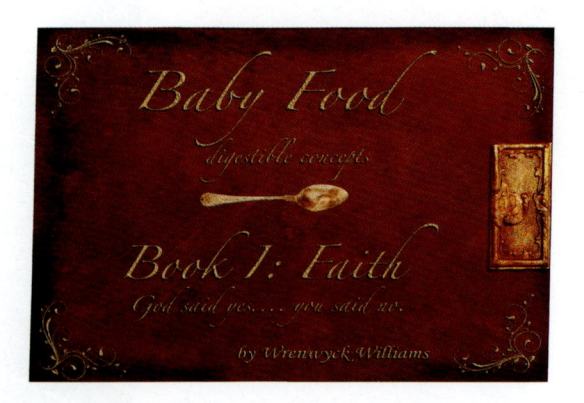